Our Alasdair

Our Alasdair

Alasdair Martin Cameron
1936~1997

A Collection of His Works
by

Ewen A Cameron

Typesetting, layout and printing by Small Print,
The Malthouse, Llangollen. Wales Tel: 01978 861990

Foreword
By Mike Harding

I was working during the summer holidays as a dustbin man in the back streets of Manchester. Two kids and a wife and a mature student degree course meant I had to hump ash cans up the slum alleys of Blackley and Crumpsal for luxuries like shoes and food. No chance of a summer holiday until Christy Moore offered me the use of a little cottage he was living in at Causeway Foot.

Somehow I managed to cadge a lift from one of the bin lads who had a car and we drove from Manchester through the Pennines to Causey Fooit as the locals called it. Christy was leaving that night but took us across the road to the pub to meet 'the locals'. Dennis Sabey who ran the Topic Folk Club in Bradford was one of them the other was a bearded, bespectacled rangy guy in jeans, a lumberjack shirt, bare feet and sandals called Alasdair Cameron. After a few pints and the sing song that followed and went on into the small hours we were friends, and stayed friends for years.

For that was the way it was with Alasdair. You might not see each other for a while but the moment you met up, after the initial 'Now you owd bugger!' the time between stripped away and nothing mattered anymore. Alasdair was a true original, a true gentle man, a very funny man and a singer whose generosity with his songs means that Sammy Shuttleworth's Party and the Battle of Sowerby Brig will live on long after all of us have gone. He killed nothing and treasured everything that had true worth; friendship, song, the sea, the great outdoors. He hated anything sham and anything that struck at the individuality of all humanity. He even wrote a song about the breathalyser, not because he wanted to drive around drunk but because he thought it another example of Big Brother watching us. I remember him singing it at the Brashaw Tavern the night he wrote it and the audience falling about in tucks - laughing not at Alasdair - but with him. He was a Lord of Misrule in a land of po-faced conformers.

The past may be another country but it is a country that is peopled with giants and one of them was a giant who lived with a pianola and the damp wheezy concertina in that stone house at Pots Oven. I treasure the memory of the man and the joy he gave me. It's an old saying but none the worse for it. They broke the mould when they made Our Alasdair.

Mike Harding

Contents

Title		Page

	Title	Page

	Title	Page

Introduction

Alasdair was tragically drowned after falling from his yacht
'Le Meteque' on the river Wyre on 6 June 1997. During the time he
was missing the beginnings of a new knowledge of Alasdair by the
family were awakened - facets of Alasdair's life which were unknown
to us; the depth of his feelings about all around him; the pathos and
humour in everyday situations; the number of circles of close friends
in an extremely diverse range of interests.

Whilst we awaited news of Alasdair after he went missing - surely he
had met up with friends and was fit and well - surely there was some
other rational explanation to his dingy and life jacket being
abandoned - a series of bitter sweet events occurred. Things like
Alasdair having another great nephew; like family laughter at
Alasdair's 'getting himself organised', like the family at ease in that if
Alasdair had gone he had gone happy - well fed, well watered and
about to go aboard his beloved boat. The realization when spectacles
were found in the mud underneath his yacht 'Le Meteque' that
Alasdair was indeed no more - and finally the 'phone call saying
Alasdair's body had been found.

Then began the daunting task of clearing the effects of a man who
had little need for 'the fancy' things of life. Things like a dry room, a
warm hearth, a good kitchen, a refrigerator, a hot bath, a warm and
dry toilet space - a man who destroyed nothing, who killed nothing,
who collected and read books on many subjects, who collected
musical instruments - even although they were all (books and
instruments) destined to be ravaged by mice and dampness.
In the clearing of Alasdair's effects there was the constant battle of
'sense' over 'emotion' - should this be ditched; should that be
salvaged; should this be sold. It was not, and could not, be possible to
give everything its due desserts - it is very difficult to judge that
papers welded by dampness or half eaten by mice could contain what
we began to refer to as 'Alasdair's Gems'. Would we be judged
irresponsible for condemning a Pianola whose veneer had lifted
when the books stored on top had been removed and whose ferrous
parts had grown to twice their normal size (like arthritic joints) due

to rusting. For condemning Squeeze boxes whose bellows had been eaten and whose reeds and keys had fused together. For condemning a zither for not being able to stand 'the simple' life.

Should intimate papers from others be destroyed - could any be recorded after suitable 'anonymising'. In the event these were destroyed - perhaps others will judge this wrong in time.

All these things were felt - and some discussed - during the clearing out operation after which, reflection gave guidance to document some of the findings. So these 'Alasdair's Gems' are put down on paper. All the Gems are in Alasdair's handwriting, although attribution to Alasdair only has not been verified. Alasdair named very few of his pieces, the titles have been given by me. Irrespective of whether the quotes are by Alasdair, they are all moving, in some case irreverent, in some crude and in the odd one or two cruel. Were these the words of my brother? They remind me of some of the unsophisticated poetry from the trenches. I have documented many of these 'Gems' and have realized I only knew the person who called to my 'ground'. In the family we always referred to 'Our Alasdair' and it was only in meeting Alasdair's many friends at the funeral that it became clear that in all the different circles of friends that Alasdair had, they all referred to him as 'Our Alasdair'. So, we all knew a bit of Alasdair for our own 'grounds' - witness Mike Harding's dimension in a poem written about Alasdair -
one bright gem of a man :-.

Cragged and sour at the lane end,
Louring under grim pike and hill stump,
The trackway mingles into weeds and sodden marsh,
Dank winter's cold lies on the still of night
And in the grayness a trough runs out beneath a spring.
But one bright gem of a man burns at the lane end.
When fires growled up the range back
Our ale-armed tongues cracked out
Songs and yarns and held back the hurrying night
That battered the hill above Causeway Foot.
We saw the darkness out and better still
We looked for nothing more.

When Alasdair visited us ~ mostly for Christmas and New Year ~ he always carried a small book with him. We all assumed that his book was to hold address information and mileage information for his motorbike (Halifax to Glasgow on 6 litres!!) On Alasdair's last visit however, he had a few pages of neat hand written script which he asked me to type out on the word processor. Subsequently I found the script to be words by G K Chesterton, and found them to describe many aspects of Alasdair's beliefs and his way of life.

From *The Rolling English Road. by Gilbert Keith Chesterton.*

Before the Romans came to Rye or out to Severn strode,
The rolling English drunkard made the rolling English road.
A reeling road, a rolling road, that rambles round the shire,
And after him the parson ran, the sexton and the squire;
A merry road. a mazy road, and such as we did tread
The night we went to Birmingham by way of Beachy Head.

I knew no harm of Bonaparte and plenty of the Squire,
And for to fight the Frenchmen I did not much desire;
But I did bash their braggonets because they came arrayed
To straighten out the crooked road an English drunkard made.
Where you and I went down the lane with ale mugs in our hands,
The night we went to Glastonbury by way of Goodwin sands.

His sins they were forgiven him; or why do flowers run
behind him; and the hedges all strengthening in the sun?
The wild thing went from left to right and knew not
which was which
But the wild rose was above him when they found him in the ditch.
God pardon us, nor harden us; we did not see so clear
The night we went to Bannockburn by way of Brighton Pier.

My friends we will not go again or ape an ancient rage,
Or stretch the folly of our youth to be the shame of age,
But walk with clearer eyes and ears this path that wandereth,
And see undrugged in evening light the decent inn of death;
For there is good news yet to hear and fine things to be seen,
Before we go to Paradise by way of Kensal Green.

1   *The Cripple*
Painfully walks his frightening way
(well it's frightening for you and me).
He was a cripple
With two sticks in his hand
His feet went out
Whim! Wham!
This way that way
The feet went where they wanted
Where they could?
But the sticks went straight
the lad knew what he was doing.
He had big shoulders,
I suppose the sticks did that.

-20/3/1982

2   *Man of Willow*
You should have the joy to stand at the side
of a man made of willow.
He can bend with the wind - he can lie with the sea.
He can sleep at your side with his head on the pillow.

His mind is as free as his body can be
He does not have to be guided by moral.
He lives life by the minute and cares not for you
because there will be no tomorrow.

-17/1/1984

3   *Deafness*
I want to sing. I want to run - to blend my voice with the song.
But! I'm deaf. I can't hear myself.
How do I sound? The sounds I make, to me, are beautiful.
But! I can't hear. Does it fit? Does it feel part.?
Or should I not sing?

- Queensbury FC 7/3/1987

4   *Brits*

Here, I think, is a point to think on,
Today I heard two fellows talking.
The way they talked they were Hungarian.
Now I don't speak Hungarian
and the only way I knew this
Was that they were both speaking English.

Now the point I think we should think on is!
The Brits abroad to another Brit - speak only English
Why are other nations' people prepared to work, to learn to speak
the language of the country they live in
they speak to each other not in their own tongue.
Why will us Brits not do that?

- Lewins 1/4/1987

5   *The Loss of a Friend*

When friends go
that's a hole in your heart,
did you know?

Did you know what they take away?
They take their life
but they take some of you
because you know them, you feel them,
you see what they are
because they're a part
a part of you.

- 15/10/1976

6   *God*

Yes!
I go to church,
for God is with me.

I live and work
do what I want,
for I know that God is with me.

I can kill a dog
and drown a rat
and I know that God is with me.

But if I kill a man, a boy,
a child, a woman fair.
I wonder then if God will smile,
or do you think that God is there?

-Royal Ripponden 8/10/1976

7   *Life*

What about life?
What about me?
The things we are supposed to have.
God's things,
the things that are free.

Nothing is free.
Nothing.
Everything that goes must come.

Everything that comes,
must be worked for
everything that is worked for
Is you, is me.
We do it.
We are life.

- Royal, Ripponden 8/10/1976

8   *Idle Fate*

She whispers sweetly,
that lady named fate.
She says it so softly,
'I'll open the gate.'

You think she means happiness,
or even success,
but she's only a teaser,
have one more guess.

She's planned you some bother,
for that's how she moves,
she'll leave you in lumber
and you'll have to choose.

But find her a lover
or find her a mate.
I don't think we'd be troubled
or bothered by hate.
- Royal - Rishworth 8/10/76

9   *Birds*

How thin!
The legs of a bird.
Had you ever noticed?

They're so frail,
and fine,
and fragile.

The body that sits on the legs.
You see!
You watch!
It's so big. So plump. So great.
Compared.
To the legs.

I wonder how it is?
they support!
- Bradshaw Tavern 9/10/1976

10   Love

You know this thing called love?
You can see it, hear it
and feel it,
when you're with people.

All the time it's there.
With some, so big and clear.
Others, soft and gentle,
you could almost miss it
- unless you know.

But if you you're loved.
That is!
True.
You can see it,
even when you're not supposed to know.
Maybe it's as well,
that we have love.
- Brown Cow - Thornton 16/10/1976

11   Instant Thought Machine

The instant thought machine. That's all I desire - to be able to hold everything that comes into my mind. That's what Charlie said. He only said it because he was stalled. He was so sick of people - the way it all worked. He saw them being awful, evil - well a bit rough - to each other and he was sick. That's why he needed an instant thought machine. Because he had great ideas in his head he wanted to get out. Never mind the guy that goes out drinking and talks - and even brags- about how he gave 'her a crack' when he got home. The women that 'share it out'. They are all a part of it. Which comes first? The man who goes for ' a bit of spare' or the lass who ' shares it out'. It's all there. It's all a part. And I'm sad. I'm frightened. I really don't know what to think. What to do. What to be. I'm frightened.
- Royal -Ripponden 23/10/1976

12   *Duty*
　　　　Let's cut the shades of the night that falls.
　　　　It gives such beauties and joy and peace.
　　It gives you a sight of a life that you have not known.

　　　　You cannot see the beauties of life,
　　　　You cannot know the beauties of peace
　　because you are a man who is supposed to work.

　　　　　　You are supposed (to)
　　　　　　　You will
　　　　　　　You must
　　　　　　Make a world
　　　　　　where people
　　　　who are somehow different
　　　　　will sit on a mound
　　　　　and direct you.

　　　　　　　Will tell you
　　　　　　　will say.
　　　　　　What you !
　　　　　　　You !
　　　　　　Yes you.

　　　　　　What you can
　　　　　　what you will
　　　　　what you must do.

　　　　　　But honest!
　　　Don't you think there's a chance for us
　　　To grasp, to grip - to make a life
　　　　　to make it nice
　　　　　to make a place
　　　　where we can live.
　　　　　　　- Bradshaw Tavern 22/10/1976

13   Tower

What about the tower?
The tower the lady's locked in.
She's been put there, because,
She doesn't agree.

Agree with her father's wishes.
Agree with the way that people are.
Agree with the ill treatment,
the horror that she sees.

That's why she's locked up.
Put away. Incarcerated.
Kept away from people.

This is what happens,
when you don't do as you're told.
When you doubt 'their' way
You're not fit to be free.

You might upset everything.
It's better for them
if they lock you away.

- Sowerby Bridge 23/10/1976

14   Deafness   .

(Alasdair perforated an eardrum in a motorcycle accident when he was twenty.)

Hello!
Have you ever cried.
Have you ever wept?

Have you ever sobbed
for someone's voice
for the joy that you get from sound?
I have.

But I can't hold.
I can't keep.
I can't get a grasp
of the beauties
the joys
that sound can give.

Oh! Please, please,
please - talk.
- Pottery Cottage 24/10/1976

Tonight I began to realize
to know, to understand
what it must be like to be deaf.

Deaf! Hell! God! S . . .!
Do you know how awful it must be?
I do because, I saw it tonight.

There was him that looked like Bedford
and Basie and Sinatra and Jones.
the whole lot, they were all there.
And I couldn't hear.
I couldn't hear.
I couldn't hear a f . . . thing.

But the people
the greats
all the people that I love
all the people that I see
they were all there
I could see but I could not hear.
They were gone.
They were dead
and
I wish I could hear.
- Friendly

21

15 *Little Creature*
Poor little rabbit.
Running in headlights.
My headlights.

It doesn't know
I don't want to kill it.
I only want to be friends.

I only want to be with it
I only want to talk with it.
Hell!

I can't talk with it.
But I want to sit with it.
and feel
and know
what is life.
- Pottery Cottage 24/10/1976

16 *The Life of a Spark*
The life of a spark as it springs from a match. It falls, it dies, it's gone.
I suppose that's the way that all things carry on.
The mountains of stone that have been there so long.
The leaves of the grass that are here 'til they're brown.
The wink of an eye that turns into a frown.
All this thought, all this feeling means nothing next day.
Because life keeps a moving - it goes its own way.
- Bradshaw Tavern 10/4/1976

17 *The King*
It's so easy to think
when you're sat on your own
that you're king of all life
that you sit on a throne.

But you then move your head
when a bird whistles sharp
you come down from your dreams
you think - is that a lark?

You then gain your senses
and think who you are
and slowly it sinks in
Larks don't come up this far.

The birds that reach up
to this side of the hill
are Pewitts and Kestrels
the birds that can kill.

All this takes you back
from the birds in the air.
You pull yourself too
and your sat in your chair.

It's the step of your house
- you didn't need a chair.
But it's your own house - you're king
and you're glad that you're there.
                              - Bradshaw Tavern 15/4/1976

18   *Ambition*

Life's so sad
for the people that fall.
But yet it comes round
and it covers us all.

You can get on so quickly
If you just drift along.
If you do right with people
They'll do you no harm.

But when you start pushing
you introduce strife.
I'm sorry! My friend.
You've just buggered your life.
            ~ Moorcock 15/4/76

19   *A Poem for Jack*

Let's make a world
create a world,
make a world
for Jack to live in.

A world that's slow
a world that's peace
a world that's calm
is slow.

A world where life
is soft, it's kind,
a world that gives you a time to find,
It gives you a time to find your peace,
it gives you a time
to find your mind.
            ~ Moorcock 24/4/1976

20   *The Man in the Moon*

I went to see the Man in the Moon
and he gave to me a bloody great spoon.
He said go down to earth
and stir them up well.
Or they'll keep sinking down.
Aye! They'll sink down to hell.
            ~ Bradshaw Tavern 25/4/1976

21   *Night*

It's got peace in it, life has,
when you fall on it right.
You can normally say
it's much truer at night.

Y' see when night falls
when night throws its dark cloak
most people are sleeping
they are dreaming - they hope.

Yes, night is a villain
Yes night is so kind,
Yes night is the balm
That can give peace of mind.
-3/5/1976

22   *Hospitals*

The pain of a friend,
relation, one dear.
I'd never quite known it,
'til the day I came here.

There's a man in a bed
at the wall
down the ward.
He's not come round yet
He can't say a word.

His wife the poor woman,
is sat at his side,
she's terrible upset
but I've not seen her cry.

25

The poor woman's sat,
with a friend by her side
which must bring some comfort
but the pain she can't hide.
- Halifax General Hospital 12/5/1976
(They didn't save him.)

23   *Dreaming*

He stood on his head
with his feet held high,
he stood with his feet in the clouds.

He thought that life,
had been leading him on.
He felt he'd been given a rather rough ride.

And then with a thump
he found his nose bled,
and then he woke up! He'd fell out of his bed.
- Bradshaw Tavern 26/4/1976

24   *Sense*

I'm naive and quiet
and soft and gentle.
I suppose how I talk
folks think that I'm mental.

People look,
and they think - pretense.
But really it's not
for I sometimes make sense.
- Moorcocks 26/4/1976

25   *The Dragon*

The dragon that St. George slew,
was the brother of a friend of mine.
That is,
he was the brother of the dragon
a long time ago.
Because then!
He was living another life.

You know how it is.
You live your life.
Then you die.
You die.
And then you come back.

And it depends what you've done
this time round,
as to who or what you are
On the next time round.

You see!
Life goes on forever.

Oh!
By the way.
The dragon that George slew,
'Were a very fair lad.'
~ Brown Cow, 16/10/1976.

26   *Army*

Teach a boy to be 'army'.
Teach a boy how to kill.
They only reflect your attitude
They only reflect your will.

They have strong boots and gaiters
and their shoulders set straight.
You can lie on your deathbed
You have only to wait.

Just wait 'til your son
kills the child of your mother.
I'm sorry, my dear
For he's just shot your brother.
                    - Evan's record shop. 4/5/1976

27   *Mellowness*

So often it's quiet
when I'm stood on the hill.
The wind has fallen,
the night is so still.

It's not that I'm drunk,
I'm not even fresh.
It's just that night comes
and she throws out her mesh.

You see! On the hills
where Nature runs free.
You can stand, you can listen,
You can stand, you can see.

And that's when it's grand
when you've been on the beer.
You can sit on your doorstep,
say 'I'm happy I'm here'.
                    - Pottery Cottage 4/5/1976

28   *Simplicity*

He was simple and quiet.
He didn't need to shout.
He was going his own way
He wanted, wanted out.

You see life,
that is   people,
kept telling him how.
How he should and he shouldn't,
what he should do now.

But you see!
How he was.
He'd never needed (wanted) a shove.
He always could tell,
tell the people he loved.

He was a man of the people,
but also himself.
He was going to find peace,
but he didn't need wealth.

- Bradshaw Tavern 6/5/1976

29   *Blues*

Do you get the blues?
How come the blues?
The day has been nice
life has been kind
but..
Then come the blues.
The blues.
A mood.
A thing that comes,
I don't know why
or how.
But all you can do
is wait and hide
and hope that they'll go
away.

- Bradshaw Tavern 9/5/1976

Fine willows, new rushes,
for whom are you so green?
TU FU (AD712-770)

Long since have I marveled
how of ten thousand creatures
there is not one,
but has its own tune.
OU-YANG HSUI (AD 1007 -1072)

Though I am different from you
we were born involved
in one another.
T'AO CH'IEN (AD 365 -427).

Some people say that God lacks any concern
for leaf or flower.
The myriad - formed!
The skill that fashioned them all!
LIU K'O CHUANG (AD1187 1269).

The flying birds two by two return.
In these things there lies a deep meaning.
T'AO CH'IEN (AD 365 -427).

All things are stirring.
I have beheld them in the place where they return.
LI ERH (6th Century BC).

Flowers of all kinds
blossom one after another,
well aware that they will fall
in a little while.
PO CHU-I (AD 772-846).

Each has its season coming early or late;
but to all alike the fertile soil is kind.
PO CHU-I (AD 772-846).
- from 'National Geographic' December 1970.

31   *Moonlight*

A thin sliver of life
standing up on a clay set hill,
She's a boat
She's a soul
She's dependent on me
I hope that I have the will.
- Pottery Cottage. 1976
(Alasdair's boat 'Moonlight' sat beside the
cottage for some time whilst Alasdair
attempted to repair her. Nature beat him.)

32   *The Jungle*

He climbed to the top of a bamboo shoot,
'cos he thought it was time that he had a look.

But the stride of the colour
the noise that came too
He thought! No I don't like it.
No! That will not do.

'cos, he thought from his sight
from the noise and the bungle,
No! Bugger it Jack
I'll go back to the jungle.
- Bradshaw Tavern 7/9/1976

33   *Truth*

A seeker of truth
is a man on his own.
For the greater of people
don't want the truth known.

You see - when the truth comes
comes corruption and sin,
and the people who do it,
would rather it not seen.

So it's hidden. It's covered
It's kept from folks eyes.
It's quite easily done,
you just have to tell lies.
                    - Bradshaw Tavern 9/9/1976

34   *Deafness and Noise*
                I feel so awkward
                the noise that they make.
            It would be so easy for me,
                        me!
                    To hate.
                    - Bradshaw Tavern 9/9/1976
            Alasdair was often tortured by noises over
                which he had no control. To us this was
                            sometimes irrational.

35   *Smokeless Zone*
Oh! The sound of the wind as it sings round my head.
It brings thoughts to my body how cold is my bed?
        You see I've no fire because I've no coal.
If the gas board don't save me I'm in a 'helluva hole'.

This all comes about 'cos the department tells me.
The smoke from my 'chimnee' they don't want to see.
        But now I've no gas. No gas for my fire.
        I sit here I'm frozen - and my fate?
                    It is dire.
                    - Pottery Cottage. 9/9/1976

36   *Real Beer*

The curtain of lace
that falls down a pint
or at least down the side of the glass.
It gives you a list -
how many mouthfuls are gone.
The number of drinks that have passed.

The curtain was there
when I was a boy
because beer was as it should.
But look at a glass
with the beer of today.
You can see that it's
no bloody good.

- Brown Cow 11/9/1976

Jean Rostand.   *Kill*

Kill one - you're a murderer.
Kill millions - you're a conqueror.
Kill everyone - you're God.

Jean Rostand.

37   *The Dreamer*

The dreams of some reach back in time,
for the time they live in seems to have no rhyme.
They are out of place because their heart is free
and they cannot accept rules like you and like me.
Then again I think and I try, try to see,
I wonder perhaps if the dreamer is me?

- Royal Hotel Ripponden 17/9/1976

The bastards!
They shoved me out.

I went for a p . . .
when I came back -

What!

Someone sat in my seat.
My pint!
My pint!
Where is my pint?
Oh!
There!
Shoved down the bar.

But I'd been moved.
I'd been shoved.
I'd been shoved down the bar.
But. I didn't want to go.

I was happy.
I was alone -
but I was happy.

And then!
Some silly bastards came
and stole my happiness.

They were ignorant.
They came in and took -
they took my seat.
They took my happiness.

Christ!
I was happy.
Alone!
But happy.
Why did they come -
the pillocks,
the idiots.

Why did they come
and kill a soul?

- Royal Ripponden 8/10/1976

39   *Class*

My body is a prisoner
ruled by convention.
But my mind!
No one knows,
It is free.

You see our bodies must do
what other people say.
Or principally the man - man,
That gives us our pay.

He gives it?
He gives it?
No!
I'll not accept that.
For if we give profit,
He!
He cares not a jot.

He cares not for you.
He cares not for me.
He cares not for the beauties
that around he can see.

The beauties that <u>he</u> sees
are tied in <u>his</u> mind.
They are money and goods
and things of that kind.

They are items that belong
in a world far, far from me.
The payment I want?
To be able to see.

To see all the strange things
that come by every day.
And the 'happies'!
the 'uglies'!
Yes, I think that's fair pay.
- Bradshaw Tavern and Brown Cow 26/9/1976

40   *In my Mind*

Too much can go on in my mind.
It's too big. It's too vast.
The thoughts that come,
they jump so far.
I see something that's kind -
and I only see hate.
I see something that's awful -
and I sense and feel love.
You see there's love in what I do.
And there's hate in what I -
Well no! Not hate but maybe wrong.
You see we're all alike.
We see good and we see bad,
we see right and we see wrong.
We want the things we've never had,
but the things we've always seen.
The things that always have been there.
We can't relax enough,
we can't see the truth,
we're so mis-guided.

Yes we've lost all our thoughts.
Me'self!
I feel frightened.
I'm so sad, for I am naught.
- On a bench in Tarbert Loch Fyne 2/10/1976

41   *Jungle*

Just now and again a thought
strikes through the mind.
through the jungle,
through the awful depths of my mind.
My mind!
What is that?

The depths of my mind, what are they?
Where do they reach?
What makes me cry?
Oh! The jungle is deep.
Times, 'tis cruel.

Times it makes me want to kill.
Times it makes me want to laugh.
Times it makes me hold and love,
times it makes me still.

Times the jungle makes me know not what.
It is that I must do.
And then I fall down by your side, my friend.
I suppose I'm much like you.
- On napkin. Blue Dahlia Halifax 10/12/1976

Dainty Donkeys.

Today. A beautiful realization.
Stood on a canal bank and down the towpath came,
a child. Riding on a donkey.
There were two donkeys
only one child.

But that's not the point
The donkeys.
They walked so dainty.
I never knew donkeys
walked dainty.
But they do
Bloody lovely. Beautiful.
                    -Queen Victoria, Glasson Dock. 27/5/1995

42   *Logic*
                    Everyone dies of emphysema.
                        Well! They must do.
                    They all stop breathing,
                        Don't they.
                            - Royal Oak 31/7/1994

43   *Saint George*
            I never thought about the awfulness, the evil,
                of bullfighting, bullbaiting. Until!

            I saw a little model of a bull.
            He had a staff stuck out of his shoulder.
                        O.K. But!
            On that staff was a flag of Saint George.
                I don't know - Saint George.
            The flag of purity, the flag of righteousness.
                            Ahhmm.
                Maybe it was just their joke -
                The flag of Saint George.

        Maybe it's all right to go out and torture bulls,
                        Or us,
                    Or anything.
                    Bad scene!
                        - 8/4/1987

44   *Tobacco*

The most unreasonable behavior of people
if you ever should stop for to think
is that
why should people around you create such a god awful stink.

They pull and breathe on tobacco
and blow it all over the place.
I know I've been talking with people
They've blown the damned stuff in my face.

They do it for I know not what reason,
I wonder if they know it theirself.
But for me,
A guy called Walter Raleigh
has buggered the whole nation's health.
- Lewins 1/4/1987

45   *City Light*

Twinkle! Twinkle! Little road
As you fall your way down the black, scarred hill.

The twinkle lights your way as you go,
as you twist and torture your way below.

The lights make it easy for you.
But do they?

Was maybe life easier, kinder
when you used to have to feel?
To probe. To gently go.
Ever so soft and ever so kind.

Was it maybe easier,
in the dark
in the wild
in the peace
long ago?
- Bradshaw Tavern 20/5/1977.

46   Breathaliser

In the days before the breathalyzer
A man could drink his fill.
Now Barbara Castle tells us all
We've enough with two pints and a gill.

Some folks have taken this to heart -
It's made 'em feel right cool.
They now down two pints and a half
And then just sit and drool.

Now I'm a grimy sort miself
And I'm not made of such.
To tell me to stop at two and a half
Is asking o'er much.

I still go out and have a few.
Six, seven, eight or nine.
It all depends on the state of mi health
And whether I've got time.

One day my time will run out
and then I'll have my say.
They'll take my license off of me -
God knows how much to pay.

I'll then go out and have my fill -
Drink 'til I've had enough.
Mrs. Castle can take her breathalyzer
And shove it up her chuff.
- Circa 1969

47 *The Pendulum*

Tick! Tock!
That's the way
they normally go.
Tick! Tock!

The pendulum on the wall.
That is,
The pendulum in the clock,
The clock that's on the wall.

It's ever so steady
So even
So slow.
It's ever so easy.
Ha! Ha!

It swings
too.
And it swings
Fro.

It's ever so shiny,
brass,
and it swings.
I think it looks nice.
In fact, I envy the pendulum.
- Coach and Horses. 21/5/1977

48 *Salt*

Have you ever thought
how life would be ?
Without salt.

41

It would be a fair bugger.
It wouldn't do for me,
Without salt.

You know - without salt
We'd be done,
Aye, fair done.

We'd frizzle,
we'd fry,
And you know what?
We'd die.
                - Dutch Bar 3/6/1977

49   *Cockerels*

Why do some -
like cockerels go
Splay their feathers
make a show?
They do it when they know
They're not really free.
They do it to say -
Please look at me.
I'm lonely, I'm frightened
I don't know who I am.
I've got to show off.

Maybe someone will see me
Perhaps they will recognize.
Perhaps someone will come
and tell me.
Who I am.
                - Bradshaw Tavern 16/9/1977

50   *Fear*

What fear.
What a fright -
but I'm sorry she's gone.

She left with the night
she was gone with the sun,
as the beam
and the glint
came over the hill.
She was away
She was gone
she had had her fill.

She has gone
she's away.
But I am still here,
she has left me - alone,
with only the fear -
of being alone.
- Bradshaw Tavern. 4/1/1980

51   *Thinking*

It's not often I think
but when I do
by Christ it hurts.

You see,
when I think
I have to consider -
That is consider other people
other things.

And so then I have to
become involved.
I have to be aware,
I have to do something
or think something for
someone else.

Yes - thinking is hard
because I have to come
out of myself.

I have to open my mind
I have to come out
of the hut
that I've locked myself in.

Yes - when I think
I generally get pain
hurt, sad.

So am I evading,
running, frightened,
of facing life?
Or am I maybe lucky
that I do not often think.
- Pottery Cottage. 6/1/1980

52   *Rain*

Rain!
Soft!
Sweet!
Falls, when I am quiet.
When I sit, look out the window.
It falls.

It's soft.
It's sweet when I am quiet.
But when I'm fit and strong,
then!
The rain is hard and cruel.

So you think the rain changes.
Or is the change in I?
- Puzzle Sowerby Bridge. 11/6/1977.

53   *The Dog*

A dog!
Down there,
On the floor,
Lying,
Twitching!

What makes her go?
Why is she running,
Where is she going?
No where.
She's dreaming.
- Bradshaw Tavern 13/6/1977

54   *Living*

This was what it was
When I was living.
I saw.
I heard.
I felt.
I knew
what life was.

But now
I sit
I walk
and hear.
But I know nothing.
Because I have lost the feel.
I've lost the feel of life.
From when I stopped
cycling, walking,
working,
for fun -
Then life has passed me by.

It's left me a husk,
A waif,
A floating feather.

I have no belief,
No thought,
No idea what to do.
I've lost. I've lost -
what to do.
I must go back
to what life is about.
I must find the peace
that I used to know.

I must go back, go back
to the life that I used to know.
Try to feel the earth flow.
Perhaps I will die.
But, perhaps I will know.
- Bradshaw Tavern 14/9/1977

55   *The Little Old Man*
The little old man, with his quaint old walk.
Passes quietly through with his little white dog.
He goes through the village like many before,
He's been through one, through many a score.

He's been going for years, for ages, for eons,
He only keeps going because he is being.
He's been walking since life, he's been walking since dawn.
He's been walking 'fore Adam and his bride Eve were born.

I wonder who he is, what he is - this man that's not there.
He knows about life, he knows about care,
He's seen everything, felt it - and yet he's still here.
I wonder if.
He is
Life!
- Bradshaw Tavern 31/10/1977.

56   *Euphoria*

Hey! Euphoria.
What about me -
The one that's alone,
That cannot see.

At least.
I cannot see how to get
in a state
Where I cannot see.
You!

Yew - for - ee - aa!
You let people go.
But I wonder!
Are they free?
- Bradshaw Tavern 1/10/1977

57   *The Watchmaker*

A little old watchmaker
doing his own thing.
No need to bother about anyone.
No need anything.
No need bother.
No need to think.
Tick, tock, tick, tock.
Tock, tick.
He doesn't have to do
or think
about anything
because
tick, tock
gives everything.
Because he has seen,
He has sung, he has felt
and he has heard! Everything.
-Hall Street - opposite a Polish watchmakers. 7/12/1979.

58   *The Play*

I could enact a play,
taken straight out of life.
Taken straight from the blood
and the life of a man.

I saw it. I felt it,
I knew it was there.
I was in a pub
at the foot of the stair.

And I saw a life
that would open your eyes.
I saw a life
that showed laughter and sighs.

A play there showing
all round the year.
Y' know the man who wrote it?
They call him - beer.

- White Swan. 5/1/1979.

59   *The Fly*

Many's the fly
that crawls up the wall,
for the spider to fall
from the sky.

To cover, envelope and
smother the fly,
to cover, envelope,
make it die.

Poor fly. Poor spider
to do such a thing.
To kill a fly,
take it off the wing.

But just a minute!
Do flys have wings?
Or is it gossamer
that they work with strings.

Is that what allows them
to fly near the flame.
Perhaps the spider to them
is a game.

Perhaps to them
the spider is naught.
The spider is nothing
until they are caught.

The spider, the flame,
is nothing you see.
With the wings of gossamer
they are free.

They are free,
until they want to get caught.
Or maybe,
they don't even give it a thought.

They are free and away
until they give in.
But then they stop trying.
Well - is that a sin?
- Bradshaw Tavern 4/1/1979

60   *Lassie*

Aa wid gi'e ye the salt
tae y'er porridge.
Aa wid d'ae wi'oot fer ma'sel.
Because aa luv ye Lassie
aa dinna naa whit tae tell.
Aa luv ye

but aa dinna naa ye
aa dinna naa whit tae say.
Aa can only say aa luv ye.
Will ye come wi me today?
- Da Cammillo 7/12/1979

61   *Who decides?*
Where lies the joy in living?
If I have anything to give
how do I know?
How do I give?
What does it mean?
To give.

Do I need to be given?
Do I need help?
Should I be given to?
Rather than me
than I
should give?

Do I need help
rather than give that help?
Who decides who it is that helps?
Who says,
'Look at that pitiful bastard.
Go! Go! Go and help him
her
it
go!
and help.'

Who, my friend,
says, 'Go and help.'?
Who.
Says 'Sit and do nothing,
and wait.'?
Who?.
- Pottery Cottage. 16/11/1979

62   *Ring the Bell.*

Ring me the bell,
Aye! Ring it. Ring it.
Ring me the bell,
to show me the way.

Ring me the bell,
It sounds so clear.
But the sound doesn't show me
where to, from here.

~ circa 1979

Contradictions .

63   *Please Call*

Would that someone would come.
That someone would call
and say hello.
And say can I come in.
Can I be near you?

To share my peace,
to share my fright, my fear.
To share my love,
to share my need.
Will someone come
and share my need?

I need you. I need her.
Need him. Need it.
I need someone, or something.
I know that I need.
But what.
What is it.
I need?

-Pottery Cottage 16/11/1979

64   *Please Don't Call*

Just like a cat.
All alone in front of the fire.

Alone.
And dreaming.

That's me.
And then.

Some silly b---- comes and says hello.
And wakes me from my reverie.

Damn.
I'm cheesed off.
- Bradshaw Tavern 31/10/1977

65   *Just Tears*

What is that on your cheek?
She said to the brown faced man.
Just tears. Ma'am.
Just tears.

They just come.
I don't think about them,
or want them,
or know why they're there.

They just come.
They're just tears.

Do you ever cry?
- Pottery Cottage 1/12/1979

66   *True Me*

First verse added 24/9/1975.
(My mind is like a mire of quag
or should that be quagmire,
I'm wandering in the depths below
I don't seem to get no higher.)

I want to rise above you all.
I seek a higher goal.
You all are content to be tied to life.
I seek to find my soul.

I think there is so much above.
Such things that I don't know yet.
But if I keep trying and trying yet -
maybe I will reach them yet.

I'm sure I can find the peace that comes,
the peace through being free.
If I can throw convention off
will that then be the real me?
- Ipswich 13/9/1975

67   *Sleep is Kind*

The night as it falls like a sheet of dark,
it covers us all but it leaves its mark.
'cos you can go to bed ill
with the cares of the world
hung over your shoulder just like a shroud.
But when you wake up you've found a new heart.
You can look at your troubles and make a new start.
Because of your sleep 'neath the blanket of night,
you face up to your fear and you make it come right.
- Ipswich 13/9/1975

68   *The Mat Lies.*

The cat lies on the mat!
The mat lies to the cat!
As the cat lies quietly away from it all,
the mat whispers tales that will enthrall.

Of mice and birds and fish and things.
the sort of thoughts that give cats wings.
The strength of the thighs that give such speed
that can beat all nature and pay no heed.

The mat leads the cat into far off dreams.
It lets it do things far beyond its means.
It will let it reach higher than ever before.
Then come back and lay down at its master's door.

The mat can do this to humans as well.
It will teach them to dream and they'll end up in hell.
Because of these dreams they reach higher life.
And when they wake up they are back in the strife.

- 25/9/1975

69   *Wondering*

The night is full of wandering clouds,
the mountains reach above,
and all the time a man is lying -
down in the valley's arms.

He lies there in the valleys peace,
because he's fearful of the storm,
he is frightened of the mountains
that were there before he was born.

The mountains deny all that he knows,
they defy for him to grasp.
They have peace and joy and happiness -
this is not for him alas.

He must seek his life from human things.
For that is the way he's formed,
but maybe it would be kinder,
if that he'd ne'er been *borned.*
- 22/9/1975

70   *The Old Dungeon Gill*

A long low room, with the beams hanging low,
they hung like the brows of Judas.
But when people came in they stole all the peace,
and the happiness left somehow.

The long low room was at peace with itself,
it was quiet just being alone.
But when people came in with so many of tales,
that brought on a terrible frown.

It just wanted the quiet, it wanted the peace,
it just wanted to be itself.
I wonder if that's why some fella's go out
and just want to drink by themselves.
- Langdale 22/9/1975.

71   *Maybe Life*

The night is like an orphan,
a wandering in the dark.
It doesn't know where to wander,
it feels it has no heart.

It wanders here, it wanders there,
it doesn't know where it's wrong.
And all the time it's whispering,
a slow but painful song.

It's crying softly for some warmth,
from Sun or Motherkind,
it needs the warmth for happiness,
it needs love to ease its mind.
                    - Bradshaw Tavern 26/9/1975.

72   *Show Him the Way*
The old man stood in the corner nearby,
he looked on us all with a cankerous eye.
He looked with an eye that was sad, bad and mean.
He'd forgotten the word happiness and what it could mean.

The life that he'd known had been hard as a child.
He'd grown up mean; he'd grown up wild.
He'd done many things that he'd rather not say,
and he'd always had bitterness right up to this day.

I looked and I wondered - could I give him help,
could I get near him, let him look at himself.
How bitter and awful was his outlook on life,
could I help him relax and escape from his strife?

Could he ease could he bend,
could he listen to me.
Could I show him the way for to set his heart free.
I had only one example, the example was me.
                    -Brown Cow Thornton 27/9/1975.

73   *City Blues*
Sweet is the sound of the voice you know,
when you've been way down in the depths below,
in the depths of your soul where things look so bad,
where all you see seems to look so sad.

Where the people, the places, the things that you feel,
there's none of them seem to be just real.
They feel so distant and far away,
that it makes you think you have lost your way.

And then it comes - the voice you know.
It straightens your back and you say hello,
it pulls you back from the depths of self pity,
and you turn yourself round and again face the city.

The city that caused you the terrible sad,
the city that seemed to make all life bad.
But then you heard the voice that you knew,
and you turned and you thanked it because it saved you.
-Wine and Pizza Halifax 29/8/1975.

74   *Just Thoughts*
I'm glad there's only the moon and me,
a sittin' here looking over the sea,
'cos I was feeling so sad and maybe low,
when the moon came along and said hello.

It said hello in a way that was kind,
it was friendly and easy and really quite fine,
and the words that it said sort of eased my mind,
it was easy and happy and free.

I was happy there was only the moon and me,
we sat there fed by the peace of the sea,
and I thought to myself why can it not be,
that there's always the moon and myself and the sea.
-8/8/1975.

75   *Ramblings.*
Why today?   Have I been able to stand and see the
mountains and see the clouds as they drifted from the west. So small.
Little clusters of nothing but yet they were something. They must
have been because they were beautiful. You cannot be beautiful
unless you are something ! But then I left the clouds because the sun
was burning my back. So I walked. And then I saw the beech nuts.
Beach nuts !   I seem to remember at the age of about seven, being
shown by a teacher at school, a sycamore, an oak, an elm and a
beech. All trees. All impressive, all beautiful. But today I astounded

57

myself. I saw a nut on the ground and I picked it up - puzzled because I did not know it. But then I just looked over my shoulder and saw a tree. I did not realize but when I looked at the tree I thought 'beech', and as I walked down the road I thought 'beechnut'. I do not know how or why the association came - but it did. Without a thought. And ever since I have wondered how it was a beechnut.

Perhaps I have got out of touch with nature. When I talk about nature I think what a great little town this is. As you walk down the road it is covered with chestnut cases, and then the chestnuts - and then you have the beechnuts and the leaves of the elm and the sycamore and another tree which I do not know. A leaf like a sycamore but smaller and it is still there when all the other leaves have fallen. I wonder could it be Maple ? It reminds me of the Canadian flag.

But really, what I am saying - thinking is that I think I saw part of it as a child. I do not think there was enough, or, that I was close enough in those days to find it all. Oh my friend it is all here. No one pays any attention. It is all there to grow up with. No one tells you what it is. You just know.

-Germany 9/11/1985.

76   *Like a Songbird*
Hello there you little thing, sparkling like a little songbird.
Spreading your joy like there will be no, no, no, no, no, no tomorrow.
We need the now and then surly mouth.
We need the occasional grin.
Because we always picture you as life without any sin.
-Pottery Cottage 4/6/1984

77   *Involvement*
The life of me I want to live, I want to take, I want to give.
But now I'm in a state of unclear.
I don't know whether I need to be alone, or whether I need to be near.
I'm frightened to lose my freedom to laugh just when I want and need,
I'm frightened that I must stop and think because there's someone else to heed.

To lose my freedom when I'm not really sure if this is what I need.
I want a knight on a big white charger to take me and then I will be
freed.

-1984.

78   *Cup Overflowing*

My cup is overflowing,
I don't know where I'm at.
The man who's supposed to look after me,
Forgot to stop the tap.

My cup flows over with misery.
My heart is full of sad.
I feel that it is self pity,
and that I know is bad.

It still takes so much to clear the soul,
so much power to clear the fear.
I wonder? Shall I die alone,
because I couldn't let others near.

-Bradshaw Tavern 31/5/1980.

79   *Din! Din!*

Din! Din! Sham! Sham!
I wonder who it is I am.
You see I met a man who said I'm me.
I said I'm not because you see.

Chorus

I'm Dim! Dim! Sham! Sham!
I wonder who it is I am.
So then he tried to make me listen
to what he had to say.
because he thought he could help me
to find a better ...

Chorus

Dim! Dim! Sham! Sham!
I wonder who it is I am.

You see I'm just a 'happy'
apart from when I'm sad.
And depending how I look at life
says whether it's good or ...
Chorus
Dim! Dim! Sham! Sham!
I'm off to see my Uncle Sam!
He's the one who lives on the hill.
He's much better off than my Uncle Bill.
Because Uncle Bill's dead and lies in a hole,
that lies at the foot of the ....
Chorus
Dim! Dim! Sham! Sham!
I suppose I don't care who it is I am.
-Bradshaw Tavern 31/5/1980

80   *Don't*

Don't let the eagle bite,
Don't let the narcissi die,
Don't let the children fret,
Don't let Grannie cry.

That's too many don'ts in a night,
for a simple man to heed,
too much for his mind to grasp,
I can't do it he's sure to plead.

But give him a simple task to do,
like drink a river dry,
or jump off the steepest mountain face
to see if he could fly.

He would try, he would do his best to please,
he would do his best with a will.
But my friend you would set too great a task,
and the poor man's heart you would kill.
-Bradshaw Tavern 30/5/1980.

Friend Tonight

Who's gonna be my friend tonight,
Who's gonna be my friend tonight.
I've been traveling so long, all on my own,
that I really want, I need a friend tonight.
Chorus
Who's gonna be my friend tonight,
Who's gonna be my friend tonight.

The rain today has made me feel so cold.
The rain today has made me feel so cold.
It's chilled me to my soul.
I think I need someone to hold
Chorus
Who's gonna be my friend tonight,
Who's gonna be my friend tonight.

Where are the days I used to roam.
I remember the days I used to roam.
But now I've lost my way,
I need somewhere to stay.
Chorus
Who's gonna be my friend today, tonight, tonight
Who's gonna be my friend tonight.

The time has come the Walrus said to me,
The time has come the Walrus said to me.
The Walrus said to me - you'd better go down on your knee
and plead someone will be your friend tonight.
Chorus
Who's gonna be my friend tonight,
Who's gonna be my friend tonight.

I saw a child today beside the road.
I saw a child today beside the road.
It waved its hand to me and I thought my God you're free,
but I would still like to have a friend tonight.

Chorus
Who's gonna be my friend tonight,
Who's gonna be my friend tonight.

Who's gonna be my friend tonight,
Who's gonna be my friend tonight.
I think I've always known
but tonight I've found my home.
Chorus
Yes I think I've found a friend tonight,
. Yes I think I've found a friend tonight.
-29/10/1983.

82   *Maiden Dancing*
There stands a rose - alone in its beauty.
Over there sits a wife - her head bowed in duty.
But here I see a young maiden dancing.
The shine in her eyes like the stars above.
It does not need the old man in the corner,
to tell everyone that the maid is in love.
-Brown Cow 30/12/1983.

83   *See Me Through a Rainbow*
See me thro' a rainbow,
take the clouds from round my head.
Let the evening sun come thro',
a glowing orange red.
Chorus
See me thro' a rainbow,
come on take me by the hand.
Yes, please take me thro' a rainbow,
take me to a happy land.
Lift the colours from the flowers,
as they grow along the way,
lift them up in handsfull.
And brighten up my day.

Chorus
See me thro' a rainbow,
come on take me by the hand.
Yes, please take me thro' a rainbow,
take me to a happy land.
Lift the colours, lift the birdsong.
Give me back to happiness.
Come on - see me thro' a rainbow,
let me once again find peace.
Chorus
See me thro' a rainbow,
come on take me by the hand.
Yes, please take me thro' a rainbow,
take me to a happy land.

-18/2/1984.

84   Thoughts in Sweden

Maybe Orwell (G) was not talking about the future when he wrote 1984. Maybe he was just talking about the present. The things he wrote about in '49 were there in '49. The queuing up for things, the oppression of having to conform was there in '49 and it's here in Goteburg, Sweden in 1981. It is as tho' generally people want to be persecuted, downtrodden, made to do as they are told. Is this evolution? Is this the natural way of things?

I think that 'I' do not conform, that I do my own thing, but I never really stand far out of line. I would agree that in wild life that animals expect and look out for destruction from other animals, but it seems to me that man is the only one (animal) who will try and destroy or control the minds of his fellows. In fact the whole system seems bent on trying to destroy the ability to think.

Look at the motor cars.
All lined up.
Waiting to be devoured.
Waiting to enter the insatiable belly of the ship.

Just like the Jews.
Waiting to enter the gas chambers.
To be eaten
by a system that was corrupt,
that had lost sight of what life was.

Maybe the car ferries mean that we,
we have lost sight of what is life?
-Five weeks cycling in Sweden (1970 miles) -June 1981.

85   *Seem*

Seem! Seem!   A word on its own.
Seem! Seem!   What does it mean?
Seem! Seem!   A word from your voice.
Seem! Seem!   It gives you such choice.

It seems that she pleaded,
It seems that we heeded
It seems that they needed
To ignore what she said.

It seems when a thing is so nice to one mind,
that along comes another and says it's un-kind.
And when one says 'abolish'
another says 'keep'.
The thoughts that keep coming are getting too deep.

It seems that it's good,
and it seems that it's bad.
It seems that you would,
and it seems that you've had.

It seems that some do
and conversely some don't.
It seems some people will
and then others they won't.

Seem! Seem!   Really what does it mean?
Seem! Seem!   I feel it's unclean?
Seem! Seem!   An excuse for my kin.
Seem! Seem!   A get out for sin.
                  -Bradshaw Tavern 31/10/1975.

86   *Come Inside*
One day whilst working outside a lunatic asylum,
              I had a job at breaking stone.
       When along came a lunatic and said to me.
                'Good Morning Mr Jones.'
     How much a week do you get for doing that.
                 'Fifteen bob I replied.'
        He turned away and he shook his head,
             and this is what he cried.

    Come inside you silly bugger, come inside.
           I thought you had a bit more sense
  a workin for a living when we get it on the tick.
        Act a little silly and become a lunatic.
             You get your meals a' regular
            and a couple of suits besides.
        Fifty bob a week and no kids to keep.
    Come inside you silly bugger, come inside.

      Now the other night I had a strange dream.
               I dreamt that I had died
  when old opertunian he came knocking at the door
           with a sword as big as a scythe.
     He said this is the place for silly buggers
    Come inside you silly bugger come inside.
                        ~

When the fanfares are done,
the applause all gone.
You can find me,
here sitting.
I'm all alone.

Alone is quiet.
Alone is soft.
Alone is me.

I wonder why?
You see I love people.
I love things. I love life.
I love him and her
and you and that.
But I'm alone.

I wonder do I make it that way.
Or I wonder if God or Fate or Life
or Whatever.
Says that I am me.
I am meant. I will be. Alone.

-October 1976.

88   *Birth of a Woman*

I gave birth to a woman.
I gave her a heart.
And I gave her a soul.
I gave her the belief
that she could stand on her own.

That she had a life, a spirit
that was her own.
That she was not lost because
her man brought her down.
I showed her that she was she.
That she was her,
she was she who could face life.
That she was still herself.

I gave birth.
I showed her.
And then she said 'Goodbye.
I don't want to know you.'
-Pottery Cottage. 17/8/1980.

89   *Peace*

The pain of a word you know is unkind.
It strikes through your body - it pierces your mind.
It cuts through your heart - it strikes through your soul.
It takes away peace and it leaves you so cold.

An unkind word you can so often say,
shows an unhappy person - doesn't know the way.
Who's lost the way to find peace in their mind.
It's really so easy, you just have to be kind.
-Adega Bar, Halifax. 11/10/1975.

What means a book,
the thoughts to write?
I mean!
Why do you stop,
why do you think.
Why do you presume,
that you can give
something to someone,
or even
someone to something.

It must be nice,
to write a book -
to give someone everything,
to give everything
to give all,
let everyone come
they come
let them grasp, grasp, grasp,
at your soul.
-Bradshaw Tavern 16/10/1976.

Epilogue

I find it odd that the analytical and logical mind of a fitter and turner - for that was Alasdair's trade - could be so different from the mind required to write these 'gems'. This was however one of his hidden features. We knew that Alasdair occasionally went to the Opera or the Ballet or an Orchestral Performance. The following is a list of Companies that Alasdair worked for.

1951	Stanley Machine Tool Halifax
1958	Morris Plastics Sowerby Bridge
1959	C T Rhodes Salterhebble
1960	Wm Asquiths Halifax
1960	Stanley Machine Tool Halifax
1961	Carding Specialists Halifax
1961	Churchill Redmans Halifax
1962	Carding Specialists Halifax
1965	Warner Swathey Asquith Halifax
1968	S W Chatterton Halifax
1969	A Fielder Bradford
1969	Churchill Redmans Halifax
1971	Carding Specialists
1976	V T L Halifax
1976	James Lumb & Son Elland
1978	Halifax Tool Company Halifax
1978	John Stirk Halifax
1980	Kearns
1980	Lathe Services Brighouse
1980	Burns and Berry Bros.
1981	Wesserhutte Germany
1981	Binns and Berry Halifax
1983	Riverside Precision Eng. Sowerby Bridge
1984	Alpha Automation Bradford
1984	Clark Bros. Bradford
1984	Clorebrook Israel
1985	I S E Germany
1987	Pratt Burnerd Halifax
1990	Process Units Halifax

1990   Boxtrees Halifax
1991   Wetheriggs Pottery Penrith
1992   Retraining
1995   F H Shaw Elland.